SOFTER GOD

Poems and Divine Conversations

Carisa Downs

ISBN-13: 9798622243011
ISBN-10: 1477123456

Cover design by: Carisa Downs
Library of Congress Control Number: 2018675309
Printed in the United States of America

To my favorite one

CONTENTS

SOFTER GOD

poems and Divine conversations
CARISA DOWNS

THAT FIRST THING

That followed your first breath -
In the beginning, a cry.

Humanity:
Every participant enters by the wide gate of
Need.

Even if Eden were still softly tended,
Her gates not angel-guarded,
Don't you think that her red and purple infants would come
squealing out
Like the rest of us?

Our instinct to depend, not dark;
Our announcement – fragility! all pure.

No one teaches us how to call for help.
Nights and sleepless months pass,
And laughter must be learned with time and skill.

You, too, were like this.

In the beginning, a cry.

Dependence you knew before evil.

Where are you? Little spirit.
I call out now to that first thing
Which followed your first breath.

Soften your straightened shoulders here.

Cry,
Come,
Expect an answer.

Where are you now?
Little spirit
Come out, you -

the molded,
reliant,
adored,
fragile,
fleshy child of the wet earth.

STILLNESS

Stillness we once knew,
Our home in the womb.
Since first breaths and first lights we have not known it,
And as our feet grew they only moved faster.
Ashore, ashore.

We are all birthed into so much sound and clamor,
And we join it with our own cry and quiver.

Stillness steals upon us in sleep but we do not remember it
Our eyes, when they open,
already find it drained,
bottled, far swung by another hand.

Stillness glistens from every distance,
But who can bear up under it?
The lonely, stinging lungs of it?
The weight, the growing gills of it?

To return to that water is
To be.
Only to be.

Why should I return to such nakedness?

In this darkness my form first knew, I think then -
I knew God.

So to stillness I return.

Return with me now.

In this stillness,
Soft! listen –
Someone approaches.

SOMETHING ELSE TOMORROW

Born into the fear of death,
I tumbled from the womb
Fumbled for the remote
Turned on the Weather Channel -

Readying myself
For whatever lightning or punishment
Might strike.

Before I knew Love,
I learned to flee hell
And scorn sleep.

I crashed into Your wings
In flight from the terrors that could not
Come near You.

You lifted my chin
Back then and said,
"Little one,
You may call me Escape From Death today.
I will teach you to call me Something Else
Tomorrow."

SHARP THOUGHTS

"It is not a safe place for you to be –

In me.
I have sharp thoughts.
They could really wound you,
Could run you through."

*"Now, here, look.
You see?
You've already done that to me.*

*I Am
Forever
Okay.*

THE AUTHOR AND HIS DAUGHTER

"I tell my daughter I love her before
She knows what the words are -
Before she can speak at all herself.
She doesn't respond at all like she hears me,
But Truth, anyway, has a way of moving the mouth.
And isn't Truth best said with joy in its breath?

If I keep telling her, from sunrise to sunset,
Perhaps one day she'll say she loves me back.
I will write that day down, no doubt,
Replay the moment over and over
Her tiny mouth forming round
The words that I taught her
The air bubbling and reeling with my own
sloppy laughter

But even if not,
Even if she never does
I will always reach toward her with it, just like this.
This child I made.
I will teach her speech
By way of my own devotion
Point to a star and say "yours,"
Wake the new day and say, "for us."

GOD AND MAN ALONE

And the all-knowing God could have formed
Adam and Eve at the same second.

Could have molded the man from the soil and the breath
But left him cradled in innocent rest
Separating his rib from his own newborn side
Letting man and wife wake locked
On each other's eyes.

For God always knew that even with all Eden's delights
And with True Love Himself to walk with at twilight
That man would still long for someone more like himself
To pass the warm garden night with
And share the new thrill of life with

So God listened intently for the first of man's sighs
That he could find no twin in the water or sky
And then God said aloud what He'd always known in His thoughts
That his man wanted a match, in addition to God

So God formed her fast for man's want
As a gift
And thus man was never solitary again

But I wonder why things didn't start off that way -
Heaven trimming a shortcut, erasing the days

When God walked with his man for a few days alone
With no one's but each other's evening
Hands to hold

Could it be that God wanted man's first joyous mornings
Spent laughing and romping and
Each other adoring?

Did God record the first of man's shouts of delight
To replay for Himself while Adam slept at night?

Did a love-stricken Father count the days that were left
When his son's childlike attention
Would have nowhere else it would land?

Did he watch His boy play
And quietly plan his marriage
All the while relishing the last sunsets they'd cherish?

Knowing soon He would gladly give us one another
Helpmates and mothers
And children and brothers
But first – give us these days to set apart for our own
When earth's first loves walked new
God and man,
alone.

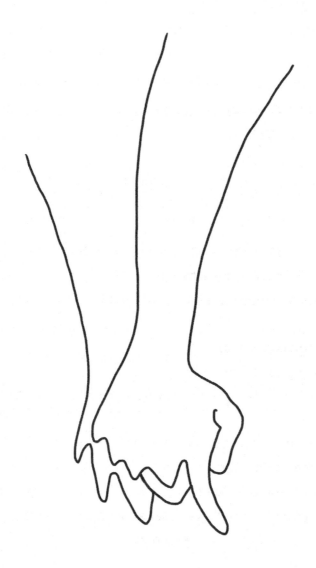

A NEW CREATION COMMENTS ON HERSELF

The list of things I would be worried about if I had a sin nature
Stays lengthy.
The length of the staff in His hand
Stays longer.

Someone said, "Be careful,
And watch your heart,
And watch your head."

I said yes and then replied, "But I, too, have the mind of Christ."

In the past
I've spent whole weeks
Pulling weeds
In soil that had no
Seeds for them.
Good fruit – it's true!
Bright, sunny-sweet
Grows in my garden now.

I see my veins.
Upturn my hands
Open my mouth
And trust my head
Like it is no longer I who live
But Holiness Himself within

EDEN CHILD

Eden child,

Breathe your Eden air
All guiltlessness and sanctity

Every breath you breathe today
First breathed into you longingly

You are a hard working child
But the earth yields for you easily

As all around creation bends to serve and listen
Close

To you, connected at the root
To the Image-bearers like you

Uncovered

Known at the eye
Knit at the soul

Is there anywhere that you could step
That would not be made safe for you?

Is there any path you'd trod today
That would not be made straight for you?

See how all you put your fingers to
Was made for you to touch

See how all your bright companions
Look like God Himself with much

Mercy

And much bravery in every
Word they speak

See how your sweet Maker
Is walking closely next to you

From your rosy waking hour
To the waning of the moon

He never leaves.
He looks at you
And you look at Him
You look more like Him every time you look
You are liked.
You are like Him
You are made for this
And are being made
Is this what it is to bloom?

THE LOVED INFANT

Observe -
She has no idea how
Each kick of her foot
Each grasping finger
So moves her mother
So floors her father

Her finite mind
Only starting to tick
Her involuntary movements
Each simply
Escape.

Nothing about her is
Planning to please
But there she is, pleasing
Ever the same.

She is a object of rapt
Awe and
Soft
Wonder
Un-asked affection
Unsought adoration

And she won't remember this, even at all.

See her start to dance
As she grows taller
Head bobbing to music

Fleshy bending and wobbling

She, with now no idea how,
All delight on each face,
The whole world is stopped
And attention is called
To record her simple
Instinctive response
To the bass, to the melody,
The beat of the drums

She doesn't pre-plan
And not much is needed
She simply is
Loved
And she has no idea

How she so moves her mother
How she so floors her father

But she won't remember this, even at all

You, little one,
When you get to Heaven
Will see how you've been
His infant
All along

Babbling and kicking
Peek-a-booing at dawn
Though you may not have felt
How you so moved His heart

You'll understand then
Though your mind couldn't grasp it
How you were, every day,
Loved more than the stars

Each grasping finger
Head bobbing to music
Your eating and falling
His delight
always were

A NEW CREATION COMMENTS ON HERSELF PT 2

Now, I am innocent
Not only in the sense that I committed crimes, indeed
And Justice chose to set me free
But now,
This innocence –
I am an infant
Who walks with sin
Like I walk with death
Which is to say, not at all

HOPEFUL, AGELESS CALL

As long as you know that you will
Always be the respondent

Not the initiate

Sigh and confess that you are
Daily
Still learning
Just to let yourself be loved
Won
Bought
Pursued and
Sought

Only then may you pursue
In turn
And seek in turn
But you must learn

That these peachy sunrises you perpetually awake to
Have always been perfumed wrists
Knocking hands
And that simply to awake is not
To open to the knocker
That the breath you are even now
Drawing in and pushing out

Was ever the "I'm here! I'm here!
Look up!"
Of God

And when you learn these foremost
Foundational things
How you'll sing
To be the response
And not the
Hopeful, ageless call

When you feel it
How you'll praise
To be the desire He attained

When you know it
How you'll thrill
To never be first
Again.

THE AUTHOR AND HIS DAUGHTER, PT 2

She tantrums in my arms.
Don't touch,
Don't taste,
No, no
I tell her.
She arches her back and wails.

If she knows that I only want to protect her,
She knows it only in some distant sense.

She insists with her fingers
Stretched toward the fiery pan
Self-assured feet
Stumbling out into the street

More ignorance than innocence
I bring her back crying.

She shrieks that I've taken from her
The very thing
She wanted the most.

She doesn't hear me
As I breathe reason into her ears, no –
Reason is above her and my voice
Is underwater.

Held tightly and safely, in-and-out breathing
Uncomforted, she pushes me away.

It pains me to pain her
But I prefer this pain
To see her poisoned.

"Know my voice," I whisper,
"And not the voice of
Death or consequence."

Relentlessly I teach her
So someday she'll love her conscience

Though she understands so little,
Perhaps she will tomorrow be
So glad
For what I kept her from today.

"I'm keeping you close.
I'm keeping you alive.
I withhold no good thing from you.
No one loves to give you what you want
More than I do."

CARRY ME CONSTANT

Will you carry me constant
Or not at all?
Life is longer than wedding bells,
And I fear that all that
Wedding bells declare
Is that someone is about to try really hard.
I have been trying for a long time.
Everything temporary disinterests me.

I will carry you constant.
What is stronger than oneness?
Between the two of us, one is trying really hard
And the other One
rests.
It is finished.
Everything eternal is yours.

FEAR OF THE SWORD

How do I stop being so afraid?

You'll have to get close to me.

But if you want to get close to me, you'll have to stop being so afraid.

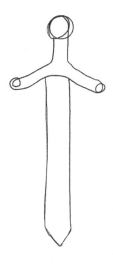

"I know that You are annoyed with me,

Because of how holy You are

And because Your sacrifice has not made me that holy, too"

Things I Used To Think, Pt. 1

MY WORST FEAR

Has always been that God is holding something against me
Something that I don't know about.
Somewhere between learning about

The Great Flood and The Rapture

I made it my job to scour the past and the present
For fragments of eggshells that I might have stepped
on

I shudder and hold them up one by one

"It's this one, isn't it?
The one that will damn me?"

Don't go cold on me.
While
All the while
My oblivious spirit slips past
You and the unknown hurt I caused
You and this unmeant sin
Don't watch me skate down some blissful trail of confidence
When hauntingly, the reality
is that You long ago went
Cold on me.

Do you look at me?

Do you tell me when I'm wrong?

Yell it at me.

Sulking
Can't be like You.

Though it may be like many mothers
Who were like their mothers, too
God, You -

You tell me when I'm wrong.

You come close
My most welcome
God-friend

When offended
You say it to my face

This relief of reliefs:
You don't go cold on me.

You, my towel fresh from the dryer.
You, the fire
You, like my cast iron
And the food in it, too

You are the heat of comfort and You consume

You,
Never cold
You,
Never cold.

GUILTY ABOUT

I told God what I felt guilty about

And as it left my lips
And touched His face
I asked, "Why don't you seem more scared?"

ICE CREAM PARABLE

Not long enough ago I dreamt
That God was a nagging husband.
He required at minimum
One hour of
Uninterrupted face-to-face time per day
Eyes looking neither to the right or to the left
Door locked
Heart rent
And if this was not satisfactorily met
He would wincingly exclaim,
"You never were mine, you idolatrous cheat!
You love all your trivialities much more than me."

Not long enough ago I dreamt
That God was neurotic,
obsessive
He could only tolerate one kind of music
During these stark, shut-in sessions
And if the tune
Dare make me
Distracted, not present
Or if my mind trailed off onto
Stray thoughts not directly pertaining to high praise
He would straightaway bolt
Wailing over His shoulder
"What a waste for a daughter,

You feeble backslider!
Now see if your hopes ever will come to pass."

Not long enough ago I dreamt
God Almighty
Was fragile.
I dreamt Him offended, perpetually.
I dreamt Him a red game
Of Russian Roulette
He might hunger for blood
He might forget my name.

I awoke from the dream that was the God I imagined
To find Him propped up in bed on the side next to me
And dotingly
He dragged my half-sleeping head
So it could sop into His chest
So my cheeks
Still warm-wet
Wouldn't ruin our pillows
And from there
He stroked my hair
And He rocked me until the shuddering
Of my shoulders had subsided enough for me to speak
And I told Him all the awful things my mind had conceived

Until He laughed
Pulled me back
To look into my eyes
Wipe away one final tear and sigh

He remembers the first time I ate chocolate ice cream
He remembers the look on my face.

LOVE AND LAW

When I read
That David said
He would not offer anything that
Cost him nothing
I began to believe that unless
It was steep
Unless I toiled hard
That God didn't much want anything
I could offer.
So my love turned to tin
When it turned into law
But perhaps love expressed is not one-size-fits-all
Love is less formulaic than I once believed.
God likes hugs in the kitchen.
God likes free.
God likes me.

God likes me ?.

MY ANCIENT MOTHER

Was removed from her garden
My fathers knew
Animal blood
Veils
The voice of their Maker through the mouths of other men.

So I was hiding on wilderness fringes
Naked, veiled, animal-blooded
When I heard the voice of the Maker
Calling out her name,
Himself.

Where are you?

The earth buckled and groaned
As God called for my mother.

Should His voice go unanswered?
How could that be?

The earth buckles and groans
Each time He speaks.

So I came, filthy and trembling,
Extending only a scarlet invitation as explanation
Between us

For this insult, this stench
That I knew I must be.

His shoulders soften.
His eyes ache.
He pulls away, unceremoniously,
My only, tattered leaf.

Are we old friends?
Have we met?

How could He? but He is,
Kneeling at my feet.

How I've missed our walks,
Our talks, Little Mother.
I've come to find you.
Come back home.

And now I walk into a mystery
Angels peer over the balcony
As I crush snake skulls with my
bare feet
And every one of them gives easily

What we have been told is true.
Yes, I am one born after the Great Death.
One of the Blessed Ones Who Can Come Back
Child of the Children Who Received the Most Excellent
Invitation

And power I didn't pay for.

Conceived on this happy side of history,
The garden doors open wide for
Me –
Someday's Eve.

KEPT

"I am able to keep you
As long as you want to be kept."

I'M IN LOVE WITH GOD AND GOD'S
IN LOVE WITH ME, A LIST

Things beloveds do:
Seize tiny moments to connect
Throw glances and leave notes
And drop hints
Prattle on about each other
All the time to everyone

Things beloveds don't do:
Count how long they have to spend time together
Before they can finally
Move on to other things
Hide from each other when they're angry or hurt
(Hiding is only to play)

I'm a friend of God and God is my friend, too

Things friends do:
Share (little things, big things, for no reason but delight)
Watch movies
Sit quietly side by side for hours

Things friends don't do:
Lock each other in rooms that they only
Open when they want to speak
Use language that they don't normally use

Just to feel heard
Beg each other to come over
When they're already
Together

MORE AND MORE AND LOUDER

I told God I wanted Him to talk affectionately to me more often.

"Come to me.
Tell me in a dream how much you love me.
I tell you all the time.
You could come to me at night, say it where I can hear you.
Why don't you?"

And I felt bitter as I asked for more,
And more,
And louder.

Open eyes, earnest brows, soft and sad.
Quietly He said, "I tell you all the time."

And suddenly in my mind's eye
I saw the unspoiled green
Of every leaf quivering in the breeze out my front window
Next, The nearly touchable
Chalk wet stripes of sunset
The skin of every hand that has touched me with
Compassion

And I said, "Oh, my God,
You tell me you love me all the time."

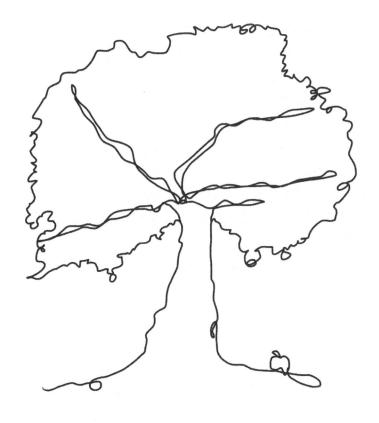

DOXOLOGY

When my mother has nestled me close
When my father has shed tears of pride
When my brothers have laughed as we played
When my husband has looked in my eyes
When my sisters have lent me their shoulders
When my leaders have laid down their lives
When a child has asked me for help
When a stranger received something kind

Always,
Ever,
Jesus,
You.

Always,
Ever,
Jesus,
You.

MERCHANT MAN

Did I know you were a Merchant Man?
Until You opened this shell
And I saw the bloom of her softness,
Her own milky labor become love-lit jewel,

I did not.

"What is it?" I ask You like we're in a dream, because I know what
it is but not why You're showing me

I ask you, "What is it?"
And You reply, "It's you."

I have always known since I was old enough to know
That I am a merchant woman.

Did I not search all my life for You?
Did I not come from far-off realms to speak to
and woo You?

Did I not allow myself to be stripped of everything,
Naked, humiliated and wounded, to win You?

Did I not, for the joy set before me, endure cost and loss
To finally call You mine?

Who is the Merchant Man
Dressed in His merchant clothes, who sold all
And gained
us?

I will ask the angels who have peered into the invisible chasms for
all of the ages till now,

Did you always know?

I am His Pearl Of Great Price.

THE KINDNESS THAT WE DON'T
KNOW WE WANT: TO WAIT

He says,
"I have much to say to you,
But you cannot bear it now."
His voice is warm milk
And He strokes my head with the flat of His
Bigger-than-me palm

I can feel that He isn't withholding
Because He thinks me weak
So much as He is waiting
Because I'm just smaller now
Than I someday will be
And many things are still
Hard for me.

I'm tired today.
But He has so much to tell me tomorrow
I close my eyes and the small words He says are grace
And the quiet between us is
Empathy

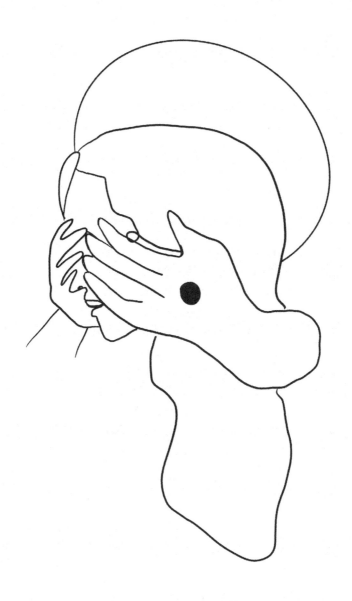

FEAR, PT 1

I knew joy and we bore art

I knew anger and we bore art
I knew grief and we bore art
I met even confusion
And we bore art
But when I knew fear, fear strangled art
In his wild panic,
tireless need to consume.
Fear and I bore survival
And survival only eats.
Eats, screams, and sleeps.
Eats, screams, and sleeps.

WORDS YOU NEVER SAID

I said to God, "I'm scared."

He responded with, "I am."
I waited for the "too,"

But it never came.

PERHAPS

When Heavenward I travel

Of me let it not be said
"Perhaps she could have rested more
And could have fretted less."

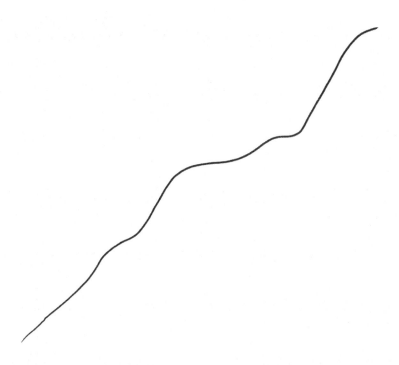

IN THE CHEST OF THE DOOR

After David raped his moonlit stranger
Murdered the man who loved them both
And cursed with death what was innocent
He said,
"Against God only have I sinned."

Perhaps the pain of God is such a vast expanse
That all other injustice is simply found in it.
When God clears the air around my face
I can see that my offenses sit only, squarely, in the chest of
The Door.

Perhaps the love of God is such a vast expanse
That all other loves are simply found in it.

If you did it to the least of these,
You did it to me.
You did it to me.
You did it to me.

FEAR PT 2

Two years ago I wrote a poem in which the character of You
laid in bed next to me
in the middle of the night, holding me tenderly as I woke from a
bad dream, wet with sweat.
Caressing, comforting me.

I cringe inwardly tonight as I think of it.

"We're not as intimate as we once were, are we?"
The realization sends me to search.
I look under my arm, behind my back,
And back at You.
I raise the other arm, look.

Where did all this fear of punishment get in
again?

WHEN THE NIGHT COMES

You will still remember
Morning stars and robin eggs
Swim through the memory of every good thing.
Say aloud, wake your spouse:
I know strawberries.
I have laughed so hard I have struggled to
Keep my hands holding those of a liar's.
Ravens have fed me by streambeds of bones
And innocent blood has made good with my belly
And I haven't been hungry in years.
All this may not lighten yet the night
But it will make it loosen its black fingers
Shush the shrieking in your mind
When morning comes
(And morning comes)
You will step outside of your upstairs apartment
Ask the world what day it will be tomorrow
They will turn to you, your brothers
And you, glistening,
Will dry your hair again from the dew.

STEAL MY PEACE

I see now that nothing
Can steal my peace.
I must choose to give it away
I must decide that it's worth the trade
Unlock it from my wrist with the key that only
I carry.

No matter how frightful the enemy,
He cannot cost me this.
My peace is either my own possession
Or it is a tragic and misplaced gift.

WHEN IT COMES TO SNAKES YOU MUST BE LOUD

When girlhood grows in the woods, it is good to have a father to teach these kinds of things.

When I walk this cold and crunching countryside now, I am caught by more thorns in my hair and my clothes than I used to be.
But this poem is neither about cynicism or the way age makes you forget.

When it comes to snakes, he said, they're more scared of you than you are of them.

I appreciate that.
I have thin, pulsing wrists.

I stomp, shout, and sing
I ask more questions than necessary of those who walk with me.

It is good to be aware of anything that would like to bite your ankles from where it lies.
But I have never been bitten.

I see them
hear me coming.
I watch them as they seek darker crannies and slide under clumsier rocks.

I survey the bouncing
red berries and the spray of
every evergreen.
The more sound I make,
the more I can look up.

OMNISCIENCE

You see everything
And that should terrify me
But your kindness
leads
And I want to be seen

WHAT THE HONEY KNOWS

To the honey I said,
"You don't know what it is
To be made of so much goodness,
Yet in a hollow be so hidden!"

To the bees I said,
"You don't know what it is
To be full of so much purpose
Yet possess no map to help fulfill it!"

To the birds above I said
"You don't know what it is
To be so masterly and gifted
Yet find no eye or ear to notice!"

And so I spun around to the orderly, joyful earth
And cried, "Oh, that your Maker were my Maker,
And your bounteous God, my God!"

To me the honey smiled,
"Yes, of goodness I know,
Though of fear, I do not."

To me the bees replied,
"Yes, of purpose we know,
But of doubt, we do not."

To me the birds spoke,
"Yes, of gifting we know,
But of pride we do not."

The earth crooned back to me,
Grew soft and buoyant beneath me,

"Oh, you are always one of us.
And it is not so hard   to be.

IF ALL'S GOING WELL, YOU'RE ONLY
GETTING YOUNGER

I said to God, "I just feel too old now."
He laughed at me
Like Sarah laughed at Him
They both heard something ridiculous.

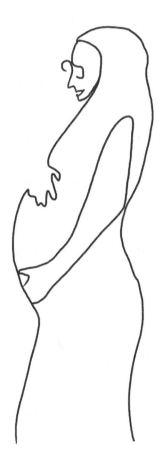

WEATHER MACHINE

There is a weather machine
Inside of me
And each day I choose
How I'll thunder through rooms
How I'll warm that one's skin
How I'll water the soils
Of the souls I will meet.
The Son rises in me
And I open my mouth
This long-awaited, piercing part in the clouds
I am lightning-handed.
And as long as I know it,
My words will drive mountains into the sea.

FAVOR & FAIRNESS

I announced aloud,
"I love my Papa so much,
I will find for Him
A spray of flowers."

I picked and plucked with my
podgy fingers
Till my doting became posies
And my devotion daffodils
My benevolence was the baby's breath
All about the bundle

I brought these to Him
With wide-eyed pride
To see Him clasp His chest
Condescend
To my height
Kiss my nose and enfold
My shoulders
Say "you are my delight" again

I think to myself that
"cost"
Is only a sound made
In a foreign tongue
That never learned the vowels of love

I would do
Anything
For this

He says to go and play
And on the way
I pass sisters and brothers
To whom it did not occur
That they should so honor and
bless our Father
with a bouquet
On this day

And I snubbed my snout
And scoffed aloud
That they should be so careless
That such neglect could run so rampant

But oh, ta-da!
Not in me, no sir
Not me

In fact
If Father should ever show favor
To one of these errants,
His children, again
I should be so confused

How not me?

How not me

A CHILD'S SERVICE

I like to serve God particular way
It's my favorite way to serve my
God
And when He wants something different from me
Sometimes, I get cross
And fuss that I want to serve Him
The way that I want
He and I both care about all of my dreams
But sometimes serving Him
Is simply more about me

DON'T JUST

Once again,

I wanted that, and You didn't give it to me.

I want to be done thrashing, resisting, and raging.

I'll still sit in your lap. Cry here
Look at your face
Tell you I love You.

You shake me by the shoulders.

Say,
"DON'T JUST LOVE ME -
KNOW ME."

My chin between your fingers
You hold my gaze.

Remind me of all the times you've done good for me before.

I watch them play in front of me,
Every
Split
Red
Sea.

I'm not just here to cry.
I know You, so I'll
Joy.
Glory.
Repent.
Rest.

HIDDENNESS & BEAUTY

So the blossom that bloomed on a green,
Empty hillside
And never knew
Admirer's face
Or the renown of standing chosen
In a lover's bouquet
Unfolded
Never wondering if she didn't deserve to be more noticed
And as she swayed, brief like a breath in the billowing empty,
She sighed and smiled
truthfully.
"Shade sometimes falls on some and stage light on others,
And many diamonds un-mined
Still shimmer all the more gladly
In the glow of their Maker's gaze."

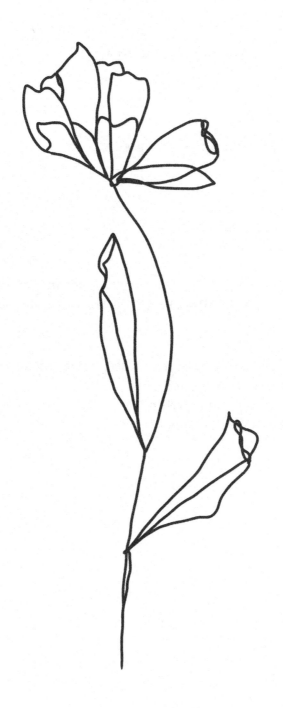

PROMISE

"It was always going to happen.
It was just about the way we looked at each other
on the way there."

PROMOTION

From where He sits near the ceiling
He pours oil and cinnamon out of a spout in His hand.

They splatter, mixed,
Into my palms, open, upturned.

I wonder what great task He anoints me for.
What holy works,
And what knowledge of my own significance will
Finally come to me
Because of this gifting, this increase,
Whatever it is.

A dull excitement stirs in me
To be
Upgraded
And as I look long into this speckled liquid in my hands
I break gaze with Him
Up there, where He is.

Stairs appear
Extending from His seat
And He walks,
A slow spiral,
Down to meet and stand with me.
Still kneeling with these oily hands

But now drawn to Him in His descent
I become thrilled with a better thrill
And I remember,
Just wipe His feet.

OTHER CHILDREN

Whenever I get jealous of those who have whatever it is that I don't / I picture their eyes glittering with hope as they look at that thing / I imagine how long they've longed after it / I envision their lips parting with an almost / unbelieving smile / as it draws near to them / And before the Great Palm can reach their tiny, outstretched ones / my mercy shouts "Hurry!" / and I share their tearful relief / as they hold that thing that we both wanted / so close / I walk from that secret window satisfied / simply that desire fulfilled / is a thing that exists / for other / cared for / children / like me.

WHEN MY HEART GOT WHOLE

Art came out

And no one had to tell me that I was supposed to write
Or sing
Or dance

I picked up the quiet leaves of my life
And said

"How did I not see,
Oh!
That you were poetry
Before?"

CITY THANKFULNESS

I have settled on a patch of land
In the city Thankfulness
And I have built a home just here
To wake up in every morning.

On the doorposts I have carved the words,
"Things You'd Be Excited About
If You Weren't Scared Of Disappointment"
And I walk through those doors every day
And I reach up and touch the letters
With my fingertips
As I go out.

I'm planting a garden in the back
And I've found out, come and see!
That the seeds that never before would grow for me
In the soil of Fear or Apathy
Burst heavy, sweetly, easily
Among Thankfulness's trees.

Breakthrough is my neighbor to my left
He loves to travel, meet new people
Giving generously without return
To those he meets along his path
But he always says that Thankfulness
So remains his favorite place

That he can't help but keep returning,
So he always circles back.

Rejoicing is my neighbor to my right
She never leaves this city's sight
In Thankfulness she was born and raised
It's as though she and this dear place
Couldn't be without the other
You could only ever meet her
If you turned to travel here
And rest your head awhile.

Down in the valleys below,
I can still see the places I sojourned
Before I decided to settle in Thankfulness
(Places like Hopelessness and Entitlement,
Self-Loathing and Self-Reliance)

And though protection and a wall against pain
Were promised by their angry gates
There's a sickness contagious in all of their streets
And I found that I suffered more within them
Than whatever I feared without

So
I climbed up the mountain
Put down my stakes
Though I put up no fences
Because Thankfulness is a place I can always leave
Whenever I want to depart

From her borders and peace

But finally,
I feel like I've tasted enough life to know
And traveled to all lesser places below
To know that I'd be a fool to ever now go
From this, my patch of land in Thankfulness.

And here I will happily lay down my head
Make my bed
And break my bread
Because Thankfulness is one of the very best things
To ever
Daily
Happen to me.

MARCHING ORDERS

I will never die
Everything in the book of my destiny
Will happen
There is nothing to worry about
I am completely provided for
All of me is saturated in love
All is well with my soul

Tell yourself these things while driving
Especially at sunset

Laugh until you cry.

VERY BUSY

I am very busy
Delighting in the Lord.
The Lord is very busy
With the desires of my heart.

THE YEAR EVERYTHING FELT LIKE A TATTOO

Commit to things
People
And places
Marry some of them
Let permanence cease to scare you
Let forever find a nest in your skin
And rest
Now certain that
You're bigger than it
You don't know if you'll always
Feel the same way about things
People
And places
As you do right now
But you know that your capacity
To keep finding good
Is great
And your capacity to
Keep falling in love

Has never been greater.

WHY I HAVEN'T BEEN DAYDREAMING
ABOUT HEAVEN

How much I daydream about heaven / and how much I believe
that I'm actually going there when I die / are probably directly
proportional / like how much I believe I am called to greater
works / and how often I command people to be healed / or the
dead to rise / like how much I have / and how much I ask / like how
much I ask / and how much I believe He'll answer / like how much
peace I possess / and how much I trust the Giver / Faith becomes
a substance / as soon as it is faith / do I daydream / command /
have / ask / possess / hope / try?

Fruit of my life, come and tell me,
frank and humbly.
Fruit of my life, come and tell me
how much faith I have.

JABEZ AND JOB

The God of Jabez is also the God of Job
And I will never understand Him.

I will know Him as I know my own face,
Yet not understand how its cells vibrate to create the form

I will be one with Him like I am one with my own skin,
Though I do not understand how each fiber of it clings
To the next
Stretches here and no farther.

I lie down in Us and know nothing but one tree,
Your sacred spillage,
And that gaping, misplaced stone.

Who is Job?
Shall I be Jabez?
Lord, what about this man
The one I know you love?

You say nothing of him or her or me
Or the differences between us or tomorrow
As it comes.
Only, "You follow me."

I know nothing but one tree,

Your sacred spillage,
And that gaping, misplaced stone.

I do not understand you.

But I know enough.

I know enough.

I know enough.

MISUNDERSTANDING

Is my least favorite of all the human disconnections.
The way it can completely miss a good heart
While still possessing such a good heart itself.

MANY ARGUMENTS & HILLS I DIED ON

The One True God
Has let me be wrong about many things.
The lack of urgency He's shown about correcting me
As I fierily raise flags
Proudly proclaim opinions
And meander about with mindsets
Has concerned me of late,
Mostly in regards to His character.
For what kind of Father would
Stand for such error?

And what kind of friend would, in error, enjoy me?

This One God of Truth
With me walks sometimes quietly.
If my thoughts are a field of
Growing things,
He takes His time plucking each single stem of
Misunderstanding from the soil.
Passing over the venom-dripping
Oleander
I only in hindsight see,
He often instead grabs for the minute spray
Of baby's breath underneath –

Conversing with me about

Much more harmless and less embarrassing things
Than that which I wish He had sovereignly

Cut out of me long ago.

Unbothered,
And bafflingly unsystematic,
He speaks to me like I'm a precocious child
Who wins Him even as she mispronounces her words.

I sometimes wonder if He doesn't
Teach me good grammar too soon
Because part of Him still loves the sound of my
Stutter

In time, faithfully
To my pain and relief
He does guide my inaccuracies
To grow into maturity

But sometimes it's like He'll almost miss
Each confident, sweet accident

THINGS I USED TO THINK, PT 2

The moment you begin some good fruit you see in yourself

Is the moment you need to balance yourself by

Remembering your weaknesses.

MY OWN UNDERSTANDING

I have this wooden staff called
My Own Understanding.
It's been with me since I was very small,
But even then,
Always,
Perpetually,
It is too short.

It's been a comfort to me
In the way familiar things are
When I have traipsed new ground
And especially when I have had to
Slog down deep valleys.
I would, especially then,
Go to lean on it
Though I knew it to be
Frustratingly small
And painful after awhile

This tilted leaning,
Leaning,
Leaning,
Always to one side.
As I grew and as I aged,

I found it even shrinking.

It's as though it started thinking
With a mind of its very own

The more weight I propped against it
The more inadequate it proved
Until, eventually
It began to trip me with hostility
Slip out from underneath me
Speak awful lies in my hearing
And I said, "This thing I thought was given me
As a leg for me to stand on
Has become my most aggressive hindrance
As I try to forward go!"

So I looked for Truth.

And the truth was told me,
That My Own Understanding
Was never made for leaning.

That it's lighter than that –
More lantern
Than crutch or life-preserver
My legs only made for
Walking by faith.
And faith always better and former,
Higher than instinct and
Hammers in the hand.

To lean on My Own, Little Understanding:

Only when I learned that this tool
Would turn against those who tried,
Did I finally shift my weight
Off of that weak and painful side.

I still take it traveling with me
Though I'm learning, slow and cautiously,
How to let it be a guide
But not the Way,
The Truth,
Or Light.

SOURCE

After you knock on the door and the man answers and says "no thank you" or "we went with someone else"

Or he says nothing at all and simply shuts the door where you stand, there remain two places in the house to which you can go.

The first is the exit. The sun cracks in every corner, and outside that door there is probably a pool, or a shaded park bench, and probably many friends. You will want to go out because you are embarrassed. You will want to go out because you have changed your mind about you and why you knocked in the first place and what reward may glitter on the other side.

And then there is the Source. This is the room you came from, but the way it feels inside and the things you knew there are often slippery and watercolor as soon as you leave. The certainties you knew in this room you may decide are false now, and then you shall go to the exit. But if you decide to return to the Source and remain, there will be the steady thrumming of what is truly true coming through all of the vents and the pipes. What you know about yourself here, what you've always known, is probably what has just been rejected at man's door. That is no matter. In this room, you are.

It is very uncomfortable. It is uncomfortable because you are very social and you really want to mingle with the man on the other side of his door. It is uncomfortable because you must often be very still here to hear what is said. It is uncomfortable because your pride is repetitively crushed in this room where no one may know who and where you are, except for the Source Himself. And it may be that some people, wonderful people, come and go while you are solitarily saturating yourself in this room's hum and thrum, and they may echo the Source's sounds with their own voices, but it will probably not be many. Though they may do their very best, they are from their own rooms, learning to turn their own dials.

After a time, you may become decent at remaining in this room for long periods, becoming quite still to hear with some accuracy. Then, you may know, like you know other certainties here, that it's time to go to the man's door and knock again.

This will be painful, I guess. It has been for me. But there may be a day when suddenly those on the other side
swing wide the door before you can lift your hand to knock. It may be that the whole world erupts into shouts, singing back to you those quiet things you've always known since you first opened your eyes.

And this will be your most conflicted moment. For all of the discomfort of the Source's aloneness and your little deaths, walking through man's door is a walk through fire. If you do it right, you'll do your business, and you'll do it for them, and you'll go as a servant, and you'll stay dead. And then you'll return to the Source.

What have you learned in all of this, going in and out among man and knocking and walking through some of them and being turned away and turning the dial and dying in secret?

With any luck, you have learned that the Source has firm floors. That there are green things growing in the walls and that everywhere else softens like sand in the hand.

HOMEMAKER

I heard you played with your mother in the water you made
I heard you played in the water with the mother you made

I heard you formed bread from air and gave it away
I heard you formed air from breath and then gave it away

I heard you wandered the roads of dust that you shook
From the comets you flung
Across skies that you painted
And made time for the questions
As well as the weddings
That you were beat till you died
But nothing could kill you

You built a house and now you live in it.
And I am the house
And I am what's living.
And though I have died, I will never die
Forever I am
both body and bride.

A HEAVEN SONG

Forever in the kingdom's courts
The tender plea
Will be heard
"Tell us again how You
Who needed nothing
Loved the slave men and women,
And longed to make them glad again."
Then, I suppose He will
Then I suppose He will.

AT THE END OF ALL DAYS

The affection of Jesus
Combs my hair with His fingers
Bundles my shoulders with His arms like
A brother
Grins at me like He's never seen anything more satisfying.
Wipes my worship-weeping with the back of a
Once-wounded palm,
I must compare You to a storm,
Storm-Calmer.

To see You is to fall face down.

To see You is to see everything else for the first time rightly.

You are the only aerial view.
I steep, I soak, I am only water.
I am a king who's heart
Is water in the hand of the King.

I am overcome.

Why would I ever leave here?
Why don't I come more often?

Why don't I just
Stay?

To worship is a stretch of every muscle.

Not because I am striving to find You anymore,
no.
But because I don't yet know how to sit in the outpour

My capacity for Love grows and grows again.
But how can my skin bear up
Under heaven?

You reserve the best wine for last.

And here, to willing spirits and weak flesh,
You give secret tastes
Of what comes after all nights
At the end of all days.

EARTHLY SISTERHOOD

Your sadness for the things that didn't happen
And your gratefulness for the things that did -
Let them now hold one another, side by side.

Let not one say to the other,
"There is no room here for you next to me."

Tonight, your gratefulness sheds a content tear
And wipes sadness's wet-lashed eye.
She does not shove and say, "Out with you, once and for all
For you are weak and I am strong."

No –
Together they go forward, embracing
Ever peaceably.

They will lie down and sleep
Warmly locked tonight

And be lit soft by
Tomorrow's dawn.

THE APROACH, ENDING WITH EXHORTATION

There is Someone who approaches you even now,
And I hope You find Him
And when I say that I hope you find Him
I mean that I hope you let yourself be taken
I hope you fling open the door to the only Door who is the One
Who has been doing the incessant knocking all this time.
When I tell you that you are loved I will also tell you that
He is jealous.

He consumes.

Even now He watches you
And I hope you know that it's time
To turn your face.
Even now.
Put this book down
And let yourself
Forever and again and again

be found.

know me know
Me know
found
me be found be
found
know me know
know me
be found
know me know
Me know
me be found be
found found
know me
be found
me be found be know
ow me know
found found
Me know
know me
be found
knowme
know me know
e be found be found be
found

ABOUT THE AUTHOR

Carisa Downs

 Carisa Downs is an author, a speaker, and worship leader, with a great love for the local Church and a great love for words and song. She is a mother to one daughter and a wife of ten years, and she currently lives in a small house in a large city where she watches the birds eat from the hanging bowl in the window as she writes - always near to family, always thinking of many friends.

Made in the USA
Monee, IL
18 August 2020